Wade In The Water

Aeriana Gallipeau

BookLeaf Publishing

India | USA | UK

Wade In The Water © 2022

Aeriana Gallipeau

All rights reserved.

Presentation by *BookLeaf Publishing*

Web: www.bookleafpub.com

E-mail: info@bookleafpub.com

ISBN: 9789357444934

First edition 2022

DEDICATION

To my younger self, you not only survive, you thrive and you shake up countless lives in the process..

~Just Like You Knew You Would~

An Ode To Those Still Standing.

Stand Proudly.

ACKNOWLEDGEMENT

Impossible Without The Most High, Those I Love, All That Have Loved Me, and All That I Have Once Been.

PREFACE

Writing is something I've always been passionate about, and as you will see I'm no scholar, I'm an Artist.

I've grappled with the idea of opening my inner workings to external observation like Willy Wonka and The Chocolate Factory for years now (Spirit got so tired of me selfishly sitting in silence).

Though many of these writings may not directly reflect me as an individual, this will be the first glimpse you get at the peculiar ways I interpret, express, and exist through this embodiment of consciousness. Here's to the first pieces of me I share, this is sacred, some of it partially channeled, all of it scribbled in a notebook my Grandmother gifted me for my 18th birthday first. Grateful to have you here for the first step on a long walk home.

The Inescapable

You don't want freedom.
    Admit you'd rather sit shackled to the light
telling yourself "We'll all break through at the
same time"

Liberation can be, and ~ I S ~ found in the
darkness you so readily run from.

There will be no Creation without confusion,
death, and deconstruction..
there never was.

The Seed Of Your Soul,
Sewn into darkness and
Sprouted Of The Same
Yet the light is overflowing with secret fear,
shame, and blame.

There exists a You
        not meant to be tamed,
  and as you've surrendered to your light....

    you will surrender again.

MAD MAN

"Close the door", he said.

Reluctantly, she does.

"Why do I listen to this MA D M AN?"
"Did you not notice you were thinking aloud?
MAD MAN, is that what you think of me; you
sure don't show that"

This one I'll keep to myself- how can I "show
that" when I'm the MAD Man too...?

"...Well maybe I'll show us both the M A D
M A N tonight."

The ~Invitation~

I think we've all seen em,
        The Gates Of Hell.
They're Breathtaking.
Rumor has it they were the gates of Heaven
itself (before Heaven got remodeled that is).
Most of us know that everything that glitters is
not gold.
So you'd think when a fine-finish, gold plated,
envelope with only the word "HELL" printed on
it showed up on my doorstep I'd throw it the
"HELL" away..
   but this is something I had been waiting on.
  It's funny how I met the Devil, to sum it up,
Whole Foods.. on the bread aisle (story for
another day).
 You see,
I know God extensively, he said this was fate,
for I had "questions the light could not satiate
and I mustn't run from this day".

Upon opening the envelope, what felt almost
like, memories flooded my mind although the
encased gilded slip was blank. Places, Faces,
Choices, and Routes leading to "The Gathering

Place", seared into the delicate flesh of my
brain,
I could never forget the way.

Forbidden Fruit

I visited that Whole Foods bread aisle two more times with hopes of running into him again. Frankly, I found it unfair that I must overcome a series of steps and obstacles just to have a conversation with a man I met so effortlessly in the grocery store.
Talk about commonly accessible yet not readily available.

    They call it "down the rabbit hole" for a reason, i heard you must descend the layers of consciousness and reality to get to his lair, and to his lair I will go....
    but I am not waiting,
  and I'm definitely not following a path forcibly imprinted onto my brain by the Devil himself.

On this side of the veil knowledge is often regarded to as the "forbidden fruit". Why, when knowledge is passed around like currency here? Beats me.
God always told me "What goes up must come down", and though I had never seen anything come down, God is no liar.

Long story short, I plan on eating red pills until
my existence as an individual ceases to exist.
Hope he doesn't mind my forced entry.

Dancing With The Devil

"You never were one to wait, I didn't actually expect you to, but I wanted to at least provide the option for a gentle arrival." -spoke a sweet, decadent, raspy voice.
The voice of the Devil, I'd known it anywhere, too good to be true.

"Never were?" I asked from the floor, head throbbing from impact, God was right, everything that goes up ~definitely~ comes down.

"You mean to tell me, you've conquered separation consciousness through enlightenment yet you don't remember the paths you and I have walked before?"- the inappropriately tempting voice responds while extending me his surprisingly mortal fashioned hand from behind an impenetrable veil of darkness.

Very suddenly music starts, a glorious song, one
we sing back home.

I reach for his hand and in between whisking me
from rock bottom and pulling me close he
murmurs the offer,-
"Dance With Me."

The Devil's "Why"

While he's clearly not known for dancing, he is impressive in his own regard I must admit.

Each step he ushers us through elegantly tracing the creation of the beat and his words keeping the rhythm.
The questions burning inside of me..
I have to know, even if just a glimpse.
Almost childishly, "What is pain?"
His words coming short at the end of mine, he now speaks sternly. "An artificially created 'weight' meant to induce the scales of distorted balance, in efforts of mimicking divine duality."

"Suffering?"
"The inevitable disintegration of our previously seated perspective of the experience."

"Why do you hate God and aspire to undermine him?"
"I don't 'hate God'. Quite the opposite actually, I admire him, even imitate my creations from the inspiration of his..
I just don't understand how he always gets it so..
'Right'. He does everything essentially perfect but I'm always one or two steps off" he admits

humbly and almost humorously. "So if one or two… or more.. people die here or there, you know, words always get distorted through the grapevine. Not saying I'm right but I'm not always 'wrong'."

The answer is unsettling. My last question triggered mostly by his self admitted admiration. "Why leave Heaven?"

"God once told me it is our choice of experience.
  Be a pawn or actively play the game yourself. Most chose the comfort of enjoying a simple interpretation of this experience to negate the uncertainty and often ridicule that comes with trusting themselves to create so fully as imperfect beings. Take note, God has started over a few times yet in his creation the actions are deemed 'Just' to an extent."

And with that the illusion of embrace with a devilishly handsome man dissipates, the music stops almost violently, and just as this strange dream begun I wearily open my eyes to what I'd just done. Slowly I reached for my throbbing head, my hand stretched over my head and into my line of sight, drenched in my blood.

Looking above, I wonder if I'll regret making a deal with the Devil to survive that jump?

Acceptance

You only want to run because you don't want to
change and you're scared of love
    Is it because love has walked out on you or
you it?

One begins to wonder
how riddles cast the scars of the heart & the stars
of the galaxy.
Is it strength that keeps us apart
  or destiny to remain afar.
Oh how these perilous words fall apart, breaking
with the chains of my heart.
Oh how the rhythm seems to come with an art,
yet the pain comes with unbearable cost.
One begins to wonder the little things that are
the tic to your clock, the drumbeat that brings
the skip to your heart, how you dance as your
mind darts to the dark, how you prance with this
oh love till depart.

Oh Love, oh weary Love, you've been here from
the start.
I've walked out on you, for I have not played my
part.

Glad We're Here

"I don't feel much anymore,
It's like the extremities of childhood emotion
have faded away.
Nowadays maybe a heavy dreary day, not
attitude filled per se,
    Just don't smile the same way."

Pain never hurts less it's just the river becomes
so vast that to float the current is easy.
There will always be rapids, but sometimes..
    ..sometimes,
Pain Feels Like A Hauntingly Present Peace.

Sometimes the road runs cold, other times it sets
you ablaze,
Let's Be Glad We're Here My Friend.

Jibber Jabber Of Writer's Block

Like any good writer I start the ritual by
lightning a cigarette, opening my journal, and it
begins.

Bursting at the seams, this time I feel it, I am
bursting at the seams.. in all aspects.
There is no right or wrong,
jumping spiders won't leave me alone
 lines I no longer want
  to write to the end
Perhaps rescuing the life of my pen
   Jibber Jabber
    Jibber Jabber
     Does it ever end?
 For sure the cigarette
   met its end
the noise too
  The only constant in my environment right
now is the pounding of a nearby basketball on
the cement…
 and even sometimes that comes to an end.

The Cicadas!….
        they never end…
until summer disappears…
  I guess every season ends.
  Is this "bursting at the seams"
            Is this my end?
Maybe I'll catch a cool breeze again..
    .. there it is.
            Every season has its
                    end
                  and yet
                every season
                  must also
                    begin.

She Was

Maybe I liked being stripped down to the
nothingness of all that I am.

and though there's a time and place for
everything, she belonged to neither time nor
place for she was not a thing.

Her existence alone was a deeply soulful
expression.
You may have found yourself in a state of awe
while standing in her essence,
for her auric field is what first announces her
presence.

She was born in the wrong day & age you could
tell by her resistance.

She allowed the years of wearing it
unapologetically to change a core component of
her delicate nature.
 She softened many bits & simultaneously had
hardened a few as well.
Her energy was intense, her capacity for
comprehension runs deep with the knowledge

she fought to fill it with. Venture through the
intricacies of her crevices,
you'll find hidden love, bold wisdom, & edgy
grace.
You'll also find sharp edged boundaries, an
unstoppable force of power, & a zeal for life it
seems impossible to match.

She built her own woman & stood strong in the
light of her aura..

From my lips, stories of her soulful nature pours
a golden liquid.

She was the remnants of the sunlight,
and the onset of the moon.

There is peace for one whose heart is open, she's
trusting that even in her darkest night this light
of love is serving her.

She Liked Poems

She liked love poems.
But she loved poems that showed you love.
  Real Love.

Like the headlights melting the night ridden
driveway.

    You don't hold onto love,
                    You Be It.

Washed Over By Love

I am washed over by love,
 I always was
Each a different cycle.

And even after all these years, the fire still burns
bright.

And even if it rains forever,
    I'll love you anyway.

It feels like the skin is melting away, each layer
revealing a different face & yet every one finds
home in the same place.

and though it'd be impossible to forget... I'll
remind myself of your face everyday.
Just as these words murmur a ceaseless cascade
So does my love accept our fade-less fate.

.... when did you first know, I've only ever
wanted to love
You.

Summer Flowers

Out of all the flowers I collected in this summer
light, your face is my favorite, though I didn't
pick it up this time.
You see some flowers I like to give a chance to
live
Especially if I don't see two of the same kind, I
let the other walk the line.

Maybe next time I'll bring a mirror with me,
pluck you out of the ground and call you mine.

These are all the things I found, last time I fell in
love with you.
I wasn't sure why I kept them.. maybe I knew I
needed proof.

This Love never lasts long.

For the bees have found flowers in which I have
grown to love,

and the buzzing of the bees is a quite important
song,
    it maybe a hint that to me you'll never belong

but I can always watch, love, laugh, and sing along.

Distorted Pleasure

Maybe I shouldn't want to destroy you with my
love. I know you would be so beautiful.

Using the word happy would be an
understatement
and who am I to understate my happiness,
        this pleasure,
 ignited by the fact that every cell was woven
together with me in mind.

Not only do we grow in love, but love grows in
me, and I know it's a long slow road to become
what you deserve..

..and in her mind, they would never meet again.

Desire

Maybe you have felt it,

    the desire to go as slow as possible....
because you already know the outcome.

    Why do we,

        not react so similarly
          to life?

Fairytale

Fairytale loves don't always have happy
endings,

    a lot of times they end in tragedy,

                even death.

Does that make the love obsolete,

    something less of a fairytale?

Coiled Seeds

The words I speak are found hard to fully interpret by the mind yet they unravel like coiled seeds planted in the seat of your soul and only in divine time.

Call To Action

No One Crowns You A Leader,

You Assume Your Position.

Fall Freely Into The Flow

They say your chances of surviving an extreme car accident are higher if you are "loose as a goose", essentially limp.

…Honestly though,

it's easier to survive this life as a whole if you are "loose as a goose" too.

 Going with whatever flow the essence of your soul moves you toward,
your path of least resistance.

While there you have time to see the sunlight peeking through the trees & slicing into the shade. You have time to smell the wild flowers or follow that butterfly that lands on you & flies off.
If you are walking against the grain of your soul (no one else's).

The path will be tough.

It's bumpy... most likely bears & stuff.

Like you're hiking through spikey balls, and
over boulders while wearing Flip Flops.

You have the option to choose wisely.
You Could Work Smarter Not Harder,

or are you going to keep forcing your essence
into a mold created to stifle every moving part of
you.

I see your soul dreaming of home.

Don't think too hard... just FLOW.

Today, Tomorrow, & Next Week.

For some reason it's always those days that the sky has gone gray that wash my sadness away.

It's like the more the weather misbehaves, my heavy energy is cleansed by the rain.

In those moments I am grateful for the day,
  as the rain rushes down my face with it it takes the pain.

I am grateful for tomorrow & the power to feel sorrow because without it our bones would be hollow.

I'll be grateful next week reminiscing on the times I felt weak because they remind us that this life is not for the meek.

Someday I pray you'll find hope in these words I speak,
 that they shine light on the path that takes you to your peak.

& Don't Forget I Am Grateful For You,

Today, Tomorrow, & Next Week.

An Ode To Myself

You will be as high as the tallest mountains you can dream of.

You can choose to frolic the valleys for all of eternity.

On the day you choose
    Greater,
        VS
          Less,

You will remember that dirt path that only you know best.

As a pleasantly inviting wind brushes past your face,
  it will carry the scent of me and you'll remember your way.

 Our destiny is calling, oh yes our journey awaits,

though waiting in angst is not really my taste.

I'm taking the path tonight and I'll do so with grace.

 I kiss you, cheeks in hand only hoping I'll remember your face..

 this time you won't see me cry so I leave in a haste

 There's days in this life I find my dial tuned to that sacred place

I don't reminisce much, I'm grateful to feel you with me everyday.

Her Divinity Unwavering & True, she moves in Simplicity with a Very Distinct Groove.
She remains Unaltered by mankind,

Her Evolution continues to run on her Own Time.

Flowing in the fact that getting Ahead often requires falling Behind.

Often noticed by Beauty, the least intriguing component of her True Physique.

Her Meticulously Crafted outer shell deters anyone not Solid enough to withstand her Flames within.

She was a Safe Place for those Wrongfully Exiled, and known as a Lock Box to those living in the dark.

The fire within her warmed those with pure intentions and scornfully seared the cheeks of those that had intentions based on fear.

She was something else.. She was Impossible to Replicate.

♡

www.ingramcontent.com/pod-product-compliance
Lightning Source LLC
LaVergne TN
LVHW010924200726
843509LV00013B/2062